Elemental Endeavors
Book 1:

fire

T. Jason Vanderlaan

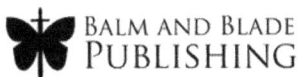

BALM AND BLADE
PUBLISHING

Fire. Copyright © 2009 by T. Jason Vanderlaan

ISBN: 978-0-9841386-0-9

Published by Balm and Blade Publishing
1475 Hollow Road
Birchrunville, PA 19421
www.balmandblade.com

Author photo by Matthew White & T. Jason Vanderlaan

Cover design by T. Jason Vanderlaan
www.jasonvanderlaan.com

~ Dedicated to my father ~

I love you, Daddy.

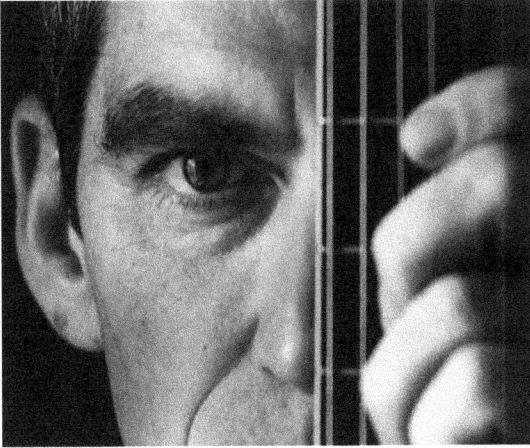

Contents

Introduction 1

Deeper.. 3

Readers, Writers, and Arsonists............................... 4

The Onrush of the Irresistible Machine 5

The Price of Fire 6

Just Before I Write.. 9

Ash and Ice 10

Walls and Open Skies.. 11

A Dark Flower Opens At Midnight 12

24 14

Tools for the Job 15

I Appreciate Your Honesty / I Hope You Will Hear Mine.... 16

The Resistance 18

Dinner at Dusk... 20

Crash and Burn 22

Rant.. 23

Girls Make Guys Stupider 24

I Wonder What Will Happen If I Push *This* Button............... 27

Paper-Thin Destiny 28

Nobody Steals Poetry Books 29

6moons5girls4clouds3charms2wishes1end0 31

Indulge 32

The Bubble.. 34

lovehateyoumyself.. 35

When He Licks His Lips, You Think It's Love 36

Epinephrine and Houseplants 37

Frozen Fire 39

Here's a Bitter Pill to Dampen the Fire of Your Holiday
Spirits (Or, Mixing Metaphors Just Might Result in a Nuclear
Disaster) 40

The Significance of My Convenience 41

My Name is in the Months 44

This One's For Free 46

They Asked For A Ballad 47

Marco Island 49

To Know You're Alive 50

Like Sheep to the Slaughter 51

Madman 53

My Apologies, Carrie, But I've Got To Say This 54

A Cure for the Common Cold 56

This is My Moment 58

Thaw 59

My Blood is Flammable 60

A Toast to Crimson Life 62

SpiritFire 63

Acknowledgements 65

About the Author 66

Fire

Introduction

I am a pyromaniac. For almost as long as I can remember, I've had a fascination with fire. So it only makes sense that as I set out to write a series of books based on the four elements, I start with fire.

There is more to fire, however, than enjoying the simple pleasures of candles and campfires. From ancient times until now, fire has evoked ideas of passion, chaos, creativity, uncertainty, possibility, and inspiration.

In Greek mythology, a distinction is made between the destructive fire of Hades and the creative fire used by Hephaestus. Similarly, in the Hebrew Scriptures, fire can either consume or purify and renew. It is this seemingly contradictory nature that makes fire so mysterious and intriguing.

For me, fire also represents a sacred longing for something more than the status quo, a burning ache for change. It symbolizes a desire for true life.

However, our search for purpose and meaning can be bewildering at times. Often it seems like we're on a hit-or-miss adventure where frequent dead ends are contrasted with rare moments when we catch glimpses of the source and fulfillment of our desires.

This is a book about that search, in all of its various complexities and paradoxes.

T. Jason Vanderlaan

Deeper

Breathe deeper,
Open up your lungs and –

This is the rush of
Totality
Bringing meaning to the emptiness.

Because you were made
For more than
Gasping though plastic bags.

So drink deeper,
Open up your mouth and –

This is the rush of
Eternity
Bringing purpose to the void.

Because you were made
For more than
Sipping life through a straw.

T. Jason Vanderlaan

Readers, Writers, and Arsonists

Sometimes rants are better written and not read,
And sometimes silence has the Midas touch.

Sometimes the folded paper
Finds its place in the pocket,
And sometimes wisdom
Is found with the teeth on the tongue.

But tables have the tendency to turn
When we least expect it.

Because the time is coming
When the voiceless will scream
And the unspoken will be heard in your ears.

And the time is coming
When the shadows will burn
And the hidden will be seen by your eyes.

The Onrush of the Irresistible Machine

I can almost feel the cogs
Turning inside my chest –
The wheels spinning
In perfect synchronization,
Whirring, purring, spurring me
On to another revolution,
Another restless resolution.

The sun rises and falls
And I concur.

Though in between I wonder
About the progression of progress
And the succession of success.

And somewhere in the distance
I hear a challenge, a command –
"Free, free! Men at last!"

But if I wait just a little longer
The voice of reason will come
To teach me reconciliation
And soothe away all my fears.

T. Jason Vanderlaan

The Price of Fire

I don't know
Which is worse:
The waiting, or the
Eternal torture of
Flesh, torn;
Liver, devoured.

But as the eagle departs
From my rock of imprisonment,
Carrying with it
The price of courage,
I know it was worth it.

They say
Hercules rescued Prometheus –
Slew the cursed Ethon,
Broke the chains
And restored freedom.

But I would forsake
Even that fortunate fate
If I could know
That fire would not die
In the hearts of men.

Fire

And they say
Prometheus was given a ring
Embedded with a piece of his prison,
To wear –
A symbol of victory
Over those who love
The cold and the dark.

And I would call myself blessed
To be so fortunate.

Just Before I Write

I can feel it in my bones,
In my blood, rushing
Through my veins
Into my arms and hands
And every fingertip –

An idea bursting forth,
Begging to be set free,
To be set down in ink.

Then a slight tremble, shudder
Of my frame
As I put pen to paper
And pour out my passion.

T. Jason Vanderlaan

Ash and Ice

In the stillness
Of a silent night
I gaze over this death field,
Covered with ash and ice,
And remember:

The lifeless cocoon
Whose occupant did not fight
For fear of flying
Into the unknown.

And in the stillness
Of a silent morning
I close my eyes,
Covered with ash and ice,
And remember:

The chaos and apathy
That engulfed this field
As green faded to black and white,
All because of one unopened cocoon.

Walls and Open Skies

Cold, concrete walls: caged
With a single dull light bulb
Hanging from the cruel ceiling.

You look at me like I'm crazy
As I begin to pound against the walls.

All you see is an open field of green,
Generously blessed by the sun's rays.

But your eyes tell only lies.
We're not free.
We're not safe here.

These walls are barriers
Between us and possibility.

Exhausted, I slump to the ground
As you tilt back your head
And smile up into the warmth
Of the flickering orb in our steel sky.

T. Jason Vanderlaan

A Dark Flower Opens At Midnight

Your petals are your shields,
Delicate and strong, but
Darker than a godless night,
Heavier than a murdered dream,
More dreary than a black sunrise.

But inside
You are the glorious heart of a rose –
Brighter than washed linen on the laundry line,
Lighter than whipped cream on cherry pie,
And more joyous than an infant's innocent laugh.

This is the mystery of you.

But they call you false,
Two-faced and double-sided.

I just think you're afraid,
Terrified that you'll open up

And they'll find you
More disappointing than rain
On what was hoped to be
A white Christmas –

A dream half-come-true,
Worse than never having dreamed at all.

I just think you're hiding.

And I am determined
To find you.

24

I've got twenty-four seconds
To show you my soul,
But in twenty-four minutes
I can hide it again.

So for the next twenty-four hours
I'll crucify my heart,
And it'll take twenty-four days
Just to make it beat again.

Because there were twenty-four weeks
That taught me to remember,
But I've got twenty-four months
I'm still fighting to forget.

And when you add it all up,
For the last twenty-four years
I've had twenty-four reasons
To make twenty-four attempts
At starting over again.

Tools for the Job

Simply put, I am exhausted
From sitting on my
Chair/couch/recliner
Staring at my
TV/laptop/monitor.

But I have just the solution.

I'll pull my .44 out of the closet
And blast a hole in the TV.
I'll rev up my chainsaw
And cut the chair in two.

I'll grab my axe
And chop the laptop to pieces.
I'll draw my katana
And skewer the couch.

I'll wield my sledgehammer
And bash in the monitor.
I'll pour my gasoline, strike a match,
And set fire to the recliner.

Then I can sigh with relief
And go take a walk outside –

If only I had the courage
To break these chains.

T. Jason Vanderlaan

I Appreciate Your Honesty /
I Hope You Will Hear Mine

Under a light in Bethlehem
You were playing your guitar –

Gold glittered from your fingers,
There was magic in your voice.
Your tunes were a true treasure,
Full of frankincense and myrrh.

Yet I cannot help but wonder:
What happens to the gifts
We don't lay before the King?

And under the glow of coffeehouse lights
In a small town in Pennsylvania,
I was listening to your songs –

I admire your courage,
And I know it takes a lot
To stand before those you love
And challenge the faith they hold.

Yet I cannot help but wonder:
Are we stronger here tonight
Or is it braver to believe?

Because you're not
The only one who struggles.

Fire

And while I may have never questioned
The existence of a face above the clouds,
I have doubted whether it had a heart of love.

Perhaps we wrestle
With the same angel.

The Resistance

This is a black night
And it's starting to absorb me,
But I'm fighting this
With everything I've got.

Because I don't want to go back
To where I lost myself.
And I don't want to become
One of the shadows again.

This is the Resistance,
And the choice must be made
To live or die tonight.

And I'll fight to the death
For life.

Fire

Dinner at Dusk

I watched the sun sink out of sight,
And thought
It must be escaping –
Running from the advancing army of the night.

She coughed,
Though not from a cold,
So I turned my eyes and thoughts
Back to dinner and my companion.

She asked me what I was thinking about.

"Oh, just about the sunset,
And our evening together,"
I said.

She smiled. Then
Frowned.

"What is that supposed to mean?"

I laughed.
"Come on, we both know why
You wanted to meet tonight.
The sun has set upon our day."

Fire

She sighed,
And rolled her eyes at my quirky grin.
"Poets are so silly.
You should just say what you mean
And leave it at that."

"But don't you see, my dear,"
I said, scooting back my chair and rising,
"That is exactly what we do.
For a fallen leaf
Cannot be described any other way."

And with that, I left.

I have an odd way
Of dealing with breakups.

Crash and Burn

I am:

f
fa
fal
fall
falli
fallin
falling
CRASH
burning
burnin
burni
burn
bur
bu
b

ashes

Rant

'Tis better to be dramatic than apathetic,
But better than both is a reason to be either.

And in the end, we're all faced with a question
That will decide the fate of our souls:

Is blood the ink
That spills from our pens,

Or are words just empty thoughts
Floating forth from the tongue?

T. Jason Vanderlaan

Girls Make Guys Stupider

So here I am, chillin' at this party,
And I'm starting to write this poem
About how I can almost guarantee
That there is a stunning inverse correlation
Between the number of girls in a room
And the collective intelligence
Of all the guys in that same room,

(Seriously, I think this can be
  scientifically proven.)

When
suddenly
another
girl
walks
in.

And my
        bro-I've-got-your-back
friends

Go into
        dude-sorry-but-you've-now-become-
        a-stepping-stone-so-if-i-have-to-diss-you-
        to-make-myself-look-better-no-hard-
        feelings-i'm-sure-you-understand
mode.

Fire

And I'm almost about to be upset,
When I suddenly realize
That all the things I used to think
Girls found repulsive
Are actually what they're attracted to!

And then this irresistible urge overtakes me,
Telling me to abandon this contemplative moment
And focus all my energy
Into putting together the most underdeveloped,
Incoherent string of words ever in the history of me

And present them to this girl
As if they're the lost words of Shakespeare himself.

Yes, now that I think of it,
This is a good plan.

She is *totally* going to fall for me.

T. Jason Vanderlaan

I Wonder What Will Happen If I Push *This* Button (F14TB06)

Today,
We will be misunderstood.
We will be analyzed and evaluated.
Judged and condemned.
Despised as love-haters
And hated as miscreants.

Today,
We will be hanged in the hearts
Of those who have determined
That love is only worth as much
As the numbers on price tags.

Today,
We will smile
Because they don't understand our joy.

T. Jason Vanderlaan

Paper-Thin Destiny

I wrap myself in a cocoon,
A wall of music, loud and chaotic.

I die to everything outside,
Losing myself in the sound
As it brings balance
And becomes my new silence.

Inside I find
Words that are my own
And yet foreign to me.

There is new blood
Beating inside my heart.

I can feel the wings
Pushing their way to the surface.

Nobody Steals Poetry Books

To be honest, I'm a little bit offended.

We've just come out of a nice Indian restaurant in Reading and there's our car: passenger window busted in, GPS stolen. I look around to see if anything else was taken. And there on the passenger's seat, beneath scattered fragments of glass, sits my copy of Billy Collin's *180 More* poetry anthology.

And yes, to be honest, I'm a little offended that the thief didn't steal it.

But I guess I understand. The GPS is worth over a hundred, the poetry book less than ten. And there's a much higher demand for an electronic device that helps you navigate the roads than for a bunch of pages with words that... do what?

I mean, I can't even make a cheesy comparison to the GPS and say that, "Poetry helps you navigate your inner life," because it's not as straightforward as that.

It's much more subtle. Poetry is less like a GPS and more like having the windows rolled down. It's less like a map and more like scenic overlooks. Less like road signs and more like the sun setting while driving on the coastline.

It is a reminder that the journey is at least as important as the destination. That life should not be lived on a turn-by-turn basis, that there is leeway for innovation, that there is time for detours. There is room for the unknown. And not only are these possibilities, they are the lifeblood our existence.

But perhaps I'm getting a little too philosophical. Maybe it's even simpler than that, like say you're walking down the street and you go past someone else's car and notice a GPS on the dashboard. Poetry is like that little nudge inside that says, "Hey, that's not mine and I have no right to take it," and so you just keep walking.

Or you look through that same window and notice a poetry book, and something inside nudges you and you're like, "Wow, I would totally love to have that book," and so you walk down to the nearest bookstore and buy a copy.

6moons5girls4clouds3charms2wishes1end0

I.
I'm testing my wings today
But that doesn't mean
I'm flying away from you.

II.
When you close your eyes,
Do I find my way inside
The life you live while you're asleep?

III.
If you wanted to be
In one of my poems,
I could have suggested
A better way.

But I bet you thought
This was about her.

IV.
Just don't mistake
This loneliness for love.

V.
I am a lighthouse –
You may see my signal
But it's not an invitation.

VI.
And now
I bite my tongue.

Indulge

Tonight I have chosen to
Indulge.

The kick of Dr. Pepper,
Rather than water.

The beat of loud music,
Instead of silence.

And, most unfortunately,
The selfish regret of a
Selfless sacrifice.

And I think:
How foolish.

But the real folly
Is that I thought this night
Could have gone
Any differently.

Because I acted as I must,
Out of love or fear,
Though it will take me a while
To figure out which it was.

The Bubble

We're just sitting around
Staring out at the world
From inside our bubble.

We are so content,
But I've got a secret
And no one knows it yet.

One day I'll rise to my feet
And get a few strange looks
As I walk towards the wall
Of our colorfully distorted views.

But no one will suspect the truth
Until I reach that horrible barrier
And pull a needle from my pocket.

Then they will hate me deeply
And glare at me viciously
As if I'm about to commit murder,

But I'll make the move
Before they can stop me:

I'll thrust out my hand,
With needle extended
Towards the unknown.

lovehateyoumyself

Do I love you?
Well, let's put it this way:
If by "love" you mean "hate"
And if by "you" you mean "myself"
Then I'd have to say yes.

Do I hate myself?
Well, let's put it this way:
If by "hate" you mean "love"
And if by "myself" you mean "you"
Then I'd have to say yes.

T. Jason Vanderlaan

When He Licks His Lips,
You Think It's Love

It's true, you're a sweetie,
But baby don't be deceived.

I see you walking around
With your soda-pop-top
And your jelly-bean-jeans,

Pursing your chocolate-chip-lips,
Fluttering your Cracker-Jack-prize-eyes.

But in his eyes you are
Just another bubble-gum-girl –

Twice the flavor, twice the fun,
But you'll still be chewed up,
Spit out, thrown in the trash
When he's through with you.

Because you see,
You're not his meal.
You're just another snack.

Epinephrine and Houseplants

Ah, sweet vicarious lungs,
Scream your songs
And share this yoke with me.

Oh, sweet perplexing peace,
Kill me, save me,
Take me far away.

You comfort me
With incarnate agony.

You join me in the grave
And carry me into the sky.

Frozen Fire

As I walk through the valley
Of the shadow of my own sins,
I fear the way this frigid night air
Can freeze my burning heart in an instant.

And I know I need Your holy fire
To melt away this bitter frost.
And I know I need Your thawing love
To free my flame to burn again.

But the distance between my head and my heart
Is farther than I used to believe
And the distance between my heart and Yours
Is farther than from here to the Sun.

So as I cry out from the depths
Of my freezing flaming heart,
I pray that You'll break these distances
Once and for all.

T. Jason Vanderlaan

Here's a Bitter Pill to Dampen the Fire of Your Holiday Spirit (Or, Mixing Metaphors Just Might Result in a Nuclear Disaster)

O Christmas tree, O Christmas tree,
Burning bright tonight
I wish I may, I wish I might
Have this wish I wish tonight.

But my lips are sealed –
Everyone knows a hope spoken
Is a dream waiting to be broken.

So blow out your candles
And I'll hold my breath.

I can hold out longer than you know.

The Significance of My Convenience

She's been talking for, like, an hour straight. I've
been listening to every word. Seriously. And
I've even been making all the appropriate
reactions, too. You know, the grunts and groans.
The perfectly timed furrowed brow and slight
shake of the head. The *hmm*'s and *ohh*'s.
Everything is going according to plan.

Just not my plan.

You see, this is the girl who broke my heart. I
know – you've heard this same sad song before.
Even for me, it's the same old, broken record.
And maybe I would let the dust gather if she
didn't keep wiping it off, putting the record back
on the machine, and dropping the needle onto that
same worn spot.

What does it mean when a girl doesn't trust you
enough to date you, but still wants to be good
friends and talks to you every week about all the
problems in her life?

I nod. Yes, that is awful. Yes, that was unfair of
him.

Maybe it's just me, but something doesn't seem
quite right about this. I don't want to be here. I
want to walk away, but I can't bring myself to do
it. So I keep listening. For my sake or hers?

41

Her mouth is mesmerizing as she lays out the details of the latest relational atrocities at her job, and for a moment I wonder if this is how an insect must feel as it flies towards the open jaws of a Venus Flytrap. But I am only a victim now if I choose to be, right? Regardless of what I think, I can see it in her eyes – she feels in control.

Suddenly her cell phone rings. She holds up a finger, not that I'd try to interrupt anyway, and turns away from me as she answer it. Her voice shifts gears from *can-you-believe-how-unfair-life-is* to *hey-baby-how's-it-going*. I wait.

She turns around. "I'm sorry, I've been talking your head off," she says, holding her hand over the cell phone's mouthpiece. "I really need to take this call."

I assure her that it isn't a problem.

"No, no. You've been really helpful, but I'm sure I've kept you long enough."

Ah, but there's the catch, my dear. You never had me.

Fire

T. Jason Vanderlaan

My Name is in the Months

I am

July, August –
    my first step is freedom from false kings and
    gods, and the assassination of a Caesar.

    you too will remember
    how the lion killed the cancer
    and the fire swallowed the water,

    but not before the ashes came to rest
    on the cities of the samurai.

And I am

September, October –
    in between I learn how to fall
    or float, as the case may be,
    but terror will answer us all,
    patriots and prisoners alike.

    and don't forget
    the day of the dead
    which teaches us all to live,
    or at least the sweet taste
    of trying not to die.

Fire

Oh, and I am

November, too –
    and I end by beginning with denial,
    refusal to give in or give up
    to an Irish winter.

    though I must give thanks
    that I am still standing
    as we struggle to remember
    the heroes who won the war
    and those who lost it.

T. Jason Vanderlaan

This One's For Free

I'm sure it must be hard sometimes
To know just what this means,
So let's try a change,
At least give it a chance –

Let's turn away from personification
As the sun turns his back on the night.

And let's put the metaphors aside
Like wedding rings in hotel bars.

Let's forget about vague phrases
Because he said she said it'd be best for us all.

And let's abandon fiction and fable,
Or at least imagine that we could.

I'd even dispense with poetry
If it wasn't too late for that.

There now.
Don't you just feel
So much better?

They Asked For A Ballad

One man standing,
Not an island,
But a tower
On an empty landscape:

Fists clenched,
Inhales –

Deep and dark
And

Screams,
Exhaling violence,
Earthquake,
Tremble
And shudder,

As windows break
The silence.

Voice forcing,
Pushing,
Breaking limits.

Blood rushing,
Flushing the face,

Crimson release
As veins burst,
Eyes roll back,
And victory is won.

Marco Island

I'm dying for some change,
So flip me a quarter
And I'll own it like my age.
I'll own it today like never before.

And I'm dying for a difference,
Two dimes and a nickel,
Because I've sown my share
And I'm just waiting for the sickle.

T. Jason Vanderlaan

To Know You're Alive

Do you need to burn
To know you're alive,
Or is it just enough to breathe
And make it through your nine-to-five?

Because
We are so afraid of
What we cannot see,

But maybe
We should be afraid
That there's nothing more than this,
That this is as good as it gets.

Because now is the time to ignite
And know that you're alive,
So take a breath like never before
And do more than just survive.

Like Sheep to the Slaughter

"I know you're a wolf."

The statement hung in the air like a noose. The only question: for whose neck?

Wolf pulled his disguise a little tighter and turned to confront his antagonist. To his astonishment, he came face to face with the shortest, chubbiest sheep he'd ever seen.

Wolf let out a low snarl. "Yeah, and what's your point? If you bleat, you'll be the first to die."

"I wouldn't make such threats, if I were you," said Sheep. "Or didn't you notice? After you came in with us through the gate, it was shut behind you."

"And?"

"And, our fences are the best in the land. You will not escape through them."

"Escape?" Wolf laughed derisively. "Who said anything about escape? I'm going to kill as many of you and your little friends as I like, eat my fill, and then slip out unnoticed with the rest of the herd when you go out to pasture in the morning."

Sheep didn't even flinch at the threat. Instead, he continued to stare down Wolf. The moonlight gleamed mischievously in his fiery eyes.

Wolf tried again. "What, are you going to get a gang of woolish warriors to try and kill me? Don't make me laugh!"

"No, they don't know about you. There is no need."

"Oh, and why is that?"

"Because I know something else that they don't know either." Sheep paused, then grinned. "Tomorrow morning, we're not going out to pasture. We're going to the slaughterhouse."

Madman

Yes, it's true:
I am a madman –

Riddle me this
And tell me the unknowable.
Decipher the code
And comprehend my mysteries.

Yes, I must be
A madman.

For only madmen
Tell parables
And expect to be
Understood.

T. Jason Vanderlaan

My Apologies, Carrie,
But I've Got To Say This

I.
Sometimes a mountain
Is a molehill.

But sometimes
A mountain is a mountain,

Sometimes
We come face to face
With Everest,

And it would be foolish
To treat it
Like a grain of sand.

II.
And what if
Jesus doesn't take the wheel?

What if the next scene
Is twisted metal
And gas-fueled flames?

Will my lips still speak praise
Even with their last breath?

Fire

Or what if I'm left alive –
And alone – to hold
The still, silent body
Of one who cannot weep with me?

Will I still find the strength to say,
"Better is one day in Your arms
Than a thousand elsewhere"?

T. Jason Vanderlaan

A Cure for the Common Cold

I.
What do you do when
Life is a boring routine
And has lost its liveliness
Like an overplayed song
Or an old, stale cracker?

II.
We all need a bit of
Constructive chaos
From time to time.

III.
So let the flames rise.
I trust that You hold
The hammer of Hephaestus,
Not the sickle of Hades.

This is My Moment

I am subversion.
I am insurrection.
I am resistance.

I am the fire
Burning at the feet
Of your straw heroes.

So remember to smile
As I throw back my cowl,
For this is the moment
When I reveal my victory.

And don't forget to laugh
As I draw my sword,
For this is my moment
And I will not stop until you see:

I am submission.
I am capitulation.
I am acquiescence.

I am the ashes
Sifting through the floor
Of your straw houses.

Thaw

Every fire I've ever lit
Has shriveled and crumbled
Into cold ashes.

But here in this desert,
You are the bush that burns
And is never consumed.

Still, I have my doubts
And wonder if You, too,
Could be extinguished.

But You remain – unchanged,
Unaffected by my icy touch –
While I, breathless, finally feel
Warmth permeating my fingertips.

T. Jason Vanderlaan

My Blood is Flammable

I've got gasoline
Pumping through my veins

And I'll give you a match,
If you dare.

But I must warn you:
My love is fierce.
My love is unrelenting.
And I will continue to burn
Once I've begun.

And we could be kerosene,
Fuel for sacred flames.

We could strike a match –
All I need is your desire.

But I must warn you:
Our love would be ardent.
Our love would be unquenchable.
And we would never cease
Once we began.

T. Jason Vanderlaan

A Toast to Crimson Life

If growing up means
Settling into cold contentment,
Then I'll bask in the warmth
Of my youth forever.

And if growing up means
Freezing my dreams in ice,
Then I'll burn in the fire
Of my imagination forever.

If growing up means
Forsaking the desire for life,
Then I'll ache in the pain
Of my passionate existence forever.

And if growing up means
Discarding hopes of adventure,
Then I'll smile in the face
Of my beautiful uncertainty forever.

SpiritFire

You've spread like a fire
Across the landscape of my soul:

A sword at Eden's gate,
The flame of Abraham's first covenant,
The holy smoldering Sinai.

And You burn me still,
Like fire in my bones,
Like flames from the sky,
Like embers on an altar.

You are
Light at my feet,
Coal to my lips,
Tongues flickering
Over my bowed head.

T. Jason Vanderlaan

Acknowledgments

Many thanks go out to Kayla McAuliffe, Matthew Lucio, and Beth-Anne White for their advice and editorial skills. I greatly appreciated your feedback as I refined this book.

I would also like to take a moment to additionally thank Lucio for all his suggestions and critiques of the cover designs for the Elemental Endeavors Series (and a variety of other projects). Although your ideas are usually too grand for me to accomplish with my skills, I appreciate how you spur me on to try new things. Without you I'd still be satisfied with using pre-loaded clipart and doodling in Paint. *shudders*

I also thank Jesus – the fire in my bones, the desire of my heart, the giver of creativity. He is the source and reason for my life. I pray that my passions will bring glory and honor to His name.

About the Author

Jason is also the author of *Unspoken Confessions*, a book that wrestles with the issues of sexual addiction, lust, dating (especially how men treat women), and purity.

More than that, it is an attempt at honesty – we all struggle with flaws of our own and with receiving the grace of God.

Unspoken Confessions is a call to find light in the darkness and to allow God to create a new heart in us as we seek to develop healthy relationships.

For more information please visit:

jasonvanderlaan.com

balmandblade.com